MW01264962

A WriteStuff Writer's Little Guide Book

A few tips that might help on your writing journey

By J. Andy Murphy

authorHOUSE™

1663 LIBERTY DRIVE, SUITE 200
BLOOMINGTON, INDIANA 47403
(800) 839-8640
WWW.AUTHORHOUSE.COM

First published by AuthorHouse 06/03/05

ISBN: 1-4208-6015-1 (sc)

Printed in the United States of America
Bloomington, Indiana

This book is printed on acid-free paper.

Dedication and Thanks...

Becoming an author was one of the biggest thrills in my life. My goal in presenting the WriteStuff Writer's Conferences and Getaway Trips was to support and motivate other writers who also dream of becoming a published author.

Love and thanks to my brother who wrote Skinny & Me from his heart and then allowed me to share it with all of you.

To Shelly Wells (shellydesigns@sbcglobal.net), many thanks for all your artistic talents in designing this book.

We all need to thank Sally Brown, co-founder of the WriteStuff Writer's and now an author, for her total commitment and support in taking us beyond where we thought we could go.

To Jean Deeds, an amazing author and one of the best teachers ever to present at the WriteStuff Writer's Getaway trips! Her book, Mountains to Climb, so electrified my life!

To all those who have attended a WriteStuff Writer's Conference, especially Laura Maria Smith, Terri LaForest, Marcia Ellett, Chris Wright, Deborah Paul, Tom Cochrun, Mike Ahern, Reed Duffy, Wendell Fowler, Larry Gilbert, Pat Finneran and Melanie Tolliver, who have now found their own way to the world of publishing. You are all my daily inspiration.

To Dick Wolfsie, my friend and fellow author. I'm proud to say I was there when your writing journey first began.

And last, but not least; to everyone who shares a passion for writing and just needs a little push to start and finish their own book!

— J. Andy Murphy

Foreword

The story of *Skinny and Me* was written by someone who woke up one morning after a terrible national tragedy with a fervent desire to share his past with his family and friends. He had no formal training in writing and crafted his words with an old typewriter using the two finger method. The story Richard K. Andersen created came from his heart and his memories. It was indeed a journey of wonderful remembrances.

Skinny and Me is a timeless story that we wanted to share with a broader audience of readers. This story was never meant to be published in a book format. It was written with the sole purpose of capturing the life of two boyhood friends and the lessons of life they shared together. It is a true story set in a time period that will never come again. We are honored to have Mr. Andersen's permission to use his prose as an example of free form writing founded in passion.

We have left his written words in his original format. No editor has applied corrections or enhanced his words or timeline process. In doing so, we leave his composition as a lesson plan for those who will spend their time trying to create their own story. We encourage you to look at this story as if you were that all important book editor carefully reading each sentence. What will you find? What, if any, composition errors are in need of correction? In other words, use this story to sharpen your proof reading skills and spur your motivation to write your own book. Remember one thing: It's easier to see someone else's mistakes than your own. This exercise should allow you to sit on the other side of the desk before you try your own hand at creating a story that takes a reader inside a world that you have created and want to share in a very public way. It should also serve as a wonderful example of writing from the heart. Not everyone writes with the idea of publishing — sometimes, though, this is the purest and sweetest writing of all.

Skinny and Me

A Simpler Time, A Simpler Life

An Original Story

By Richard K. Andersen

Prologue

For 34 years, I was a dedicated police officer. The good, the bad and the truly ugly were all part of my everyday existence. I knew from the very beginning that when a person puts on a police uniform, they're subject to a certain amount of danger and exposure. It all goes with the oath and the badge. Not every cop is a hero. But, more often than not, a good policeman wouldn't hesitate for a split second to lay their life on the line for another human being.

When I retired, I really thought that I had seen the last of evil close up. I felt safe. Content.

September 11th changed all that. Standing in a hotel lobby in San Diego early in the morning, I stood dumb-struck by the events that were playing out before my eyes on a live television broadcast from New York.

Today, I am still extremely sad, and at the same time, very angry at those individuals who answer to the name of terrorist. This group of cowards is not religious. They do not act in the name of God. Could anyone who would commit such an act be in possession of a soul?

Why would someone want to do such a horrific thing to innocent people? I cannot find an answer that lets me rest within, and so, I search for a simpler time, a simpler life.

A Dream of the Past

Last night, I had a dream that took me back in time. When I awoke, I remembered it (which is odd for me, as I usually don't). The dream was about my childhood and was centered on my friendship with my very best boyhood friend, Joe Fiscus.

When I was growing up in Indianapolis, Indiana in the l930s, it was a peaceful place – a time of innocence with limited complications. This morning, after thinking about my dream, I just felt the urge to put it all in writing and to share it with my family, especially my children and my grandkids, who unfortunately, will never know such a time.

I begin this by going back to the summer of 1939. That was the year that I met "Joe."

I was doing my usual thing as a five-year old, sitting on the front steps of our home watching the cars go by. We lived on a hill directly across from a beautiful park. Now in that time period, streets weren't as busy as they are today and there weren't a whole lot of cars passing by. Maybe that's what made it so special. When a car did come by, it was worth watching.

I remember catching the first sight of a moving van, slowly pulling up just a few feet down from our property line that was identified only by a great old oak tree with the biggest spread of branches that you'd ever seen.

The hill that our house was built on wasn't separated from the other houses like dwellings of today with concrete driveways. It was as if we all lived on one great big rolling piece of land, separated only by trees and bushes.

Pretty soon several men carrying all shapes and sizes of boxes emerged from the moving van and began to climb the three flights of steps that led up to the second biggest house on the block. By comparison, our house was a very nice, two-story double, but not nearly so large.

I was pretty excited as I ran into our house to tell my mother "someone is moving in next door!" She smiled as she handed me a peanut butter sandwich. She told me that I should go back outside and keep watching in case the new neighbors had children.

I grabbed my sandwich and headed back out to my steps. Within minutes, a black car arrived and a man and woman got out along with a boy (about 18), a little girl (about 3 years old), and lucky me, another boy that I will later discover is just four months older than me!

My about-to-be new best friend said something to his mother and immediately came running up the hill toward me. As he got closer, I could see he was a bit huskier than I was. In those days, I was a bit slim.

"Hi, what's your name?" he said, as he now stood directly in front of me a good two inches or so taller.

I immediately answered "Dick," which was a nickname for Richard.

He fired another question at me.

"What's that you're eating?"

"It's a peanut butter sandwich," I replied.

Then it was my turn to ask a question.

5

"What's your name?" I said with a small smile.

"Joe," he answered, staring at my hand, which still held my lunch.

Never one to be a bit shy about food, Joe quickly stated that he was hungry and that my sandwich sure looked good. It seems with the move and all, Joe had missed his lunch.

Without thinking, I gave Joe the other half of my sandwich. Like two little guys who knew each forever, we went off to play cowboys. When you're a kid, formalities are unimportant. It's what you have in common at the time that counts. Joe and I had cowboys in common on that day... and oh yes, a peanut butter sandwich.

This was the first day of a friendship that would last over 60 years.

When the world seemed a lot safer and I was young...

A lot of my dream recalled the times Joe and I spent playing in Spades Park that was across the street from our homes.

Today, the rose bushes that once lined the gravel walking paths are gone. Several of the biggest trees have disappeared, and the manicured grass is deeply worn in huge areas, but it's still there ... serving as a neighborhood park even after all these years.

Now our park didn't have all the things like major parks of today have, but it was big enough to have a lot of adventures in and helped to create many neat memories for two little guys always looking for excitement.

In fact, it's been said that John Dillinger once sat at a certain picnic table in Spades Park and planned a bank robbery a day before he actually did it. The facts are that a bank robbery did take place in our city, and John Dillinger was the bank robber! Whether or not Dillinger occupied one of our picnic tables can't really be documented in any way, but it served for many spirited discussions between us kids. Anyhow, that's part of our park's history.

Yes, Spades Park was a special gathering place in the neighborhood where everyone would celebrate the 4th of July and many other special holidays. Lots of family events took place in that wonderful and peaceful park. Times when people came together to talk, play games, and just wonder at the passing sights. I have to admit that as a kid, I never looked at the park across the street from our house as anything special. Today, as part of my past, I realize how lucky and blessed I was to have such a grand place to tread upon. Always there. Always waiting to be used. Always welcoming our presence as visitors.

One of the things I remember most about the park was its neat shelter house. It was round and open on all sides with eight big gray pillars holding up a huge roof. It came complete with two public restrooms that you had to go down a flight of steps to visit. It was a dark, damp, smelly place down in the basement of that shelter house.

"They say that everyone has their own 15 minutes of fame. Well you know, my mother told me that when I was about two years old I won a "baby contest." (can't even imagine that, but everyone says it's true) that was held one summer's night. The Park's Department had sponsored it all, and mom did indeed enter me in the "Spades Park Cutest Baby Contest."

Years later, Mom would show me the picture of the silver cup that was presented to her as the contest prize. I asked her if they gave me a personal prize and she said, "No, the cup was all that we got." Hmm? I somehow wonder about that!

I'm not sure whatever happened to that silver cup, but everytime I hear the song "Baby Face" I remember the look on my mother's face the day we shared this conversation. It's a small connection to make, but then sons do have certain memories of their mothers. This is one of mine."

7

Our mothers always told us that if we had to go to the bathroom to make sure we came home. It was rumored that there were creatures living down there that would hang around waiting for kids to come in so they could grab 'em.

Funny how you hear mothers talking and then come away with your own impression. Well, it worked. Come hell or high water, none of us neighborhood kids would ever use the park's restroom, even if it meant nearly wetting your pants racing to get home to a safe and sound bathroom.

On those rare occasions when Joe and I had too much liquid stored in our bladders, we would be lookouts for each other and just find a big old tree to baptize! Now that was considered "daring!"

At the edge of the park, there was a small creek (Pogue's Run) with a narrow walking bridge that connected the far side of the park with our neighborhood. Often, when it rained, the banks would overflow (sometimes five or six feet above the normal level); but mostly, it was just a small, pleasant stream.

Joe and I spent many a day playing in it; making rafts and floating our boats, always wondering if we let it go, where would the boat wind up? In the big river, or maybe even the ocean? The world was so mysterious back then. But in our imaginations, nothing was impossible. Curious little guys, we were.

When neighbors really knew each other...

Another fond memory of growing up on Nowland Avenue was the tradition that after dinner, practically the whole neighborhood would come out and sit on their front porches. Everyone would talk to each other, shouting across the verandas to be heard. Joe and I loved this because it meant that with our families all front and center, our pleas for more playtime would be granted.

As it would begin to get dark and the sky went from blue to purple, one by one, all the kids would go in separate directions to get home before it became black as pitch. Time to leave the great park; time to get away from the mosquitoes, time to sit on our porches again and watch the fireflies (lightning bugs), time to enjoy our great homes and our gathered families.

My dream brought back the memories of Joe's big front porch (or veranda as some call it). Joe's father installed a swell swing that was held in place by chains connecting it to the high ceiling of the porch. We had so much fun on that swing. It was especially memorable on rainy days when we just sat there playing our games, or swinging together talking about this or that.

I also won't forget Joe's mom saying to us one day, "Don't swing too high or you'll hit the window!" Guess what? Fate was to meet those words. We did hit the window and her warning became a "happening."

Uh-oh, we were in trouble, but only for a short time. Mrs. Fiscus was a woman of words, but a gentle soul and not one to take up with much action. The window got fixed the same day, and we were right back swinging, talking and laughing again that evening.

Funny what you start to recall when you go back to those childhood memories. Even after all these years, I can still remember the rain racing in the gutters anchored to our house. The swift waters came flowing out of those gutters like a waterfall during a storm. Our storm sewers weren't so great in those days, so a good rain would almost always cause minor floods to occur in the street out front. Sometimes we were able to talk our parents into letting us go out and play in the water. We would even lay down and let the rain water flow over our bodies. Being kids, we didn't even think about all the debris and other stuff that might have been passing over us as we laughed and splashed, pretending to be swimming in a raging river. It was great fun, and especially so, since there wasn't much traffic on our street and this was as near a swimming pool as we were to experience in our time.

I remember another day when a group of us decided to play in the park's shelter house on a gloomy day. Things were going along okay when all of a sudden we were caught up in

9

one of those quick and unexpected summer rainstorms. As a kid, I didn't pay much attention to the sky and even though the clouds changed from blue to a dark gray, the rain was always just a bit of a surprise to me. Within a few minutes, a lot of water began building up around the shelter house. Then, what seemed to come from nowhere, a giant bolt of lightning hit a nearby tree. Almost immediately, branches from the wounded tree came crashing down on top of the shelter's roof. We all had big, bulging eyes from the flash of the lightning bolt and the incredible sound of the thunder jolt stunned our ears as the branches hit directly above our heads.

"Scared stiff" took on a new meaning to us kids. Without much hesitation, some of the other kids started talking about the "what ifs?"

What if the shelter fell down?

What if the creek became a raging river and trapped us?

With each new "what if?" the situation grew darker and darker in my eyes.

That's when Joe said, "Dick, if the creek overflows much more, we'll just grab a log drifting by and we'll float across the street to our own yard."

I never stopped to think about the fact that I had never seen any logs drifting around before in a rainstorm, but Joe was older and he knew what to do. I listened to him and I really thought this was a good plan and just might work. I was afraid, but I wasn't alone. Joe was there and we had a plan. Oh, the minds of young innocent kids!

All ended well that day because in about a half-hour the storm subsided and the rising water began to pull back. Believe me, Joe and I made a mad dash for our homes before more rain came. We didn't want to be involved in another lightning show in the sky. I'll bet we broke the record for the 100-yard dash that day.

It was a wonderful storm. It made me realize how big and powerful Mother Nature can be when she lets go.

Under one roof...

Neighborhoods are made up of many different families. Joe and I had families that were very different. At my house, we had a lot of people living all under one roof.

Our family consisted of my dad, Olav, who came to the USA from Denmark at the age of 18. Dad didn't know many words in English when he first arrived in America, but he quickly learned enough to get by.

Dad was sponsored by a Danish family that lived in Detroit. They helped him secure a job working on an assembly line at an auto plant. Before he could really get settled in, there was a huge layoff and he was without a job. That's when Dad decided to join the United States Army. He liked serving his new country so much that he spent most of his life in the

Jeannine Marie and Richard Kent

military. I don't think I ever met another person who was as patriotic as my father.

There was also my mother, Myrtle. She met my father in 1933 when she went to a dance that was held downtown at the Indiana Ballroom. It was Halloween night and indeed they danced the night away. Less than two months later, they were married. In 1934, Richard Kent Andersen was born. That would be me!

The matriarch of our house was my grandmother, who we called "Remy." Remy's daughter from her second marriage also lived with us. Her name was Mary Alice and she was my youngest aunt.

My great aunt Myrtle (my grandmother's sister and for whom my mother was named) completed the family circle. Years later, in 1942, my baby sister Jeannine was born.

Yes, our house was a bit crowded, but we had many good times under that shared roof. And as I remember, Joe also spent a pretty fair share of his time there too! At dinner time for instances we would all sit down to eat together, and just like clockwork, Joe would show up at our back screen door with his nose pressed against it asking for me.

Of course, mom would ask him if he had eaten, and his stock answer was, "Yes, but I'm still hungry." Joe would be ushered in and seated next to me at our table with the family. Mom knew Joe always had plenty of food at home, but he just enjoyed eating and being with us. (Plus, I think he really enjoyed my grandmother's cooking.)

Sometimes my mother would shoo him away because she knew I would eat whatever was on my plate, like it or not, just to be able to go outside and play with my friend.

I think sitting down to dinner together, as a family is really an important part of a child's development. Families don't do it so much anymore especially with the hectic schedule of today's life. Television and computers also distract a family and this simple gesture of coming together to share a meal and conversation doesn't seem to have the importance that it once did in today's society.

I really do believe that kids quietly observe and important values are developed while sitting at the right hand of a parent as you pass a bowl of vegetables or mashed potatoes around that family table.

For instance, I remember a particular habit my dad had in regard to eating. At times, Dad would pile all his food on top of each other on his plate. I thought that was disgusting. He'd just say "it all goes to the same place." As for myself, I was always neat about the food on my plate; potatoes here, meat there. Nothing was allowed to touch. Dad would always look at my neat plate and give way to a half-smile. We were different in this way, but it was okay.

I learned a great deal from those family moments. It gave me an opportunity to see my family as real people. Not just a mom or a dad, or an aunt, or a grandmother. I heard them tell jokes, sing songs, talk about their day. I could sense that they loved each other and that they really enjoyed being in each other's company. If there was a disagreement, they would argue, but it would be in a manner that didn't scare me. I learned how to agree and to disagree from watching them. I learned a lot about life sitting at that very wonderful kitchen table for so many evenings of my life.

I miss it. I miss their company now that they are nearly all gone. My sister and I are all that's left of that close knit family unit, as all the rest are now in a better place. Absent in person, but never in spirit or memory.

When you get older, memories come back at odd times. Every year, as the seasons change, I'll start to think about my most favorite time of the year. It's always the same — winter in the park.

As a kid, it was the best time of the year (summer was good, too, but winter was better) for Joe and me. My dream brought back several of those moments when Joe and I had snowball fights, made snow castles, angel wings and fun shapes.

Today, when I watch the movie "Christmas Story," I always reminisce about growing up during this simpler time. It's like this movie was a page out of our lives (Joe's and mine). The way the boys dressed with the pulled down ear flaps on their caps, the scarves, leggings, and plaid overcoats. I can vividly remember looking out the front window and seeing the first winter snowstorm settling in with the snowflakes glistening on the ground like little diamonds. The park lights made it look like a beautiful winter wonderland. I'd get kind of possessive about the snow in the park, thinking that I didn't want anyone to walk on it until I did it first! Joe and I would call each other on the phone the moment the snow started coming down heavy with a promise to meet at the street as quick as we could.

Typical kids, we'd always hoped that school was going to be canceled because of the snow, but usually, it was not. I also warmly remember that on these snowy occasions, most of the neighbors would join us outside for a walk through the park. It was great, not really cold, but crisp.

Then we'd all go home and have some hot chocolate and climb into a waiting warm bed. Lying in bed, I would fall asleep thinking about what we'd do in the park the next day. Yes, snow falling meant a great deal to me as a kid. It's sad that as adults we forget what fun a really great snow brings. But then, I guess I don't remember my father shoveling the stuff either. I never remember him saying anything bad about snow. Coming from Denmark, he was really used to the cold and snow (maybe snow was in his blood). I remember him throwing an occasional snowball at us and how red his cheeks got in the cold. I wish I could ask him now how he really felt about snow, but these are things a kid never thinks about until it's too late.

When I think about the holidays...

Christmas at our house was quite special. Mom took so much time meticulously decorating the house, and the tree was always so beautiful. She created a wonderful miniature village that was always present beneath our tree. Homemade ceramics houses and small figures and cars were fixed to look like a neighborhood all nestled beneath our tree in a winter wonderland setting. Today, my sister and I keep this tradition alive with our own little Christmas tree villages. We each have inherited certain pieces of Mom's original set and over the course of time, have added many new features to it. Traditions – they come from family.

Another thing I remember so clearly about the Christmas season were the great aromas that came drifting out from the kitchen. Mom and Remy and Aunt Myrtle were all great cooks. I can almost still smell the likes of their fresh cookies, cakes, pies, and candy. And oh that wonderful Christmas meal!

My sister and I were lucky; we received a lot of presents. We weren't wealthy (no one in the neighborhood was either), but we had a comfortable, nice life. Yes, Christmas morning was super... so special.

I remember that I could hardly wait until the hour was decent to call up Joe so that we could compare what we had received as gifts from Santa Claus.

Something that now stands out in my memory is the fact that whatever the size of my cowboy gun, Joe always seemed to get a bigger one! And, sometimes, he would even get a double holster set! The only thing better than one six-gun was two of them.

Joe and I never had a problem sharing and playing together with our toys. We would strap on the six shooters and head outside to get all the bad guys (we'd always win, of course). I can still see us running up and down the alley out back of our homes just wearing ourselves out playing. Oh, how I miss those extraordinary moments.

Our war...

Sunday, December 7th, 1941 was a day that really changed all of us from my generation. I remember sitting on the floor playing with my toy soldiers when the phone rang. My dad answered it. It was Joe's dad on the other end asking if we were listening to the radio because Pearl Harbor had just been bombed. We didn't have the radio on, but when mom heard dad's remarks she turned it on immediately. I could tell by my family's reaction that this was something very serious. I had never heard of Pearl Harbor, but I listened anxiously to all that was being said. The next day, dad came home from work early. There was good reason; he had re-enlisted in the U.S. Navy. When he told us what he had done, my mom began to cry. Instinctively, I knew she was scared. I was too.

A few days later, mom and I went to the train station to say goodbye to dad. There were so many other men (fathers, brothers and sons) at the station with their families. Everywhere you looked there was a lot of hugging, kissing and crying. It really didn't sink in right then that my dad might not return to us. As a child, you never imagine something like that could happen to a parent. It was such a sad day for so many people. Little as I was, I could sense it all had a purpose. Our fathers were going away to protect our country.

Joe's older brother, Raymond, also enlisted in the U. S. Army as a medic. Several months later, Joe's family was notified that his older brother had been wounded in Italy and would receive a Bronze Star for his bravery under fire. A few days later, the Fiscus family would place a white star in their front window. This was the custom for families whose sons had been injured in the war. Little did I know then, that soon, both our homes would have a star hanging in the front window.

From that the day on, Joe and I piled on the guns and became back yard commandos. We landed on make believe beaches, stormed bunkers, destroyed the enemy in hand-to-hand combat. We never lost a battle. When we got wounded, Joe's little sister, Karen, would bandage us up and give us Kool-Aid. Then off we'd go to another battle.

One day after supper, I was sitting on the front steps when a small black car pulled up, and what seemed to me to be an old man (about 60) got out and came up the steps holding an envelope. He asked me to get my mother. I did, and when she came to the front door, he handed her an envelope. Even before she opened it, she seemed to know why the man was there.

I remember my Mom making a strange sound. Not a scream, but a very deep moan that sounded like "oh no." Then Remy came out on the porch and took the telegram away from my mom who was now in a kind of shock. Remy read the telegram out loud.

"Your husband, Chief Petty Officer Olav Andersen, has been wounded in the Fiji Islands and is now being transferred to the San Diego Naval Hospital..."

I don't remember the rest of what my grandmother read. Shock is not limited just to adults. My dad was hurt. That's all I could handle at that moment.

As soon as they heard the news, Joe and his mom came over to comfort us. Joe stayed the rest of the day with me. As we walked over to the park, we said all those brave things that made us feel bigger like, "we'll get even."

That was a long day for two little guys to get through who were both hurting in their own way. Fear was also present that day, though neither of us said the word out loud.

Several weeks later, we were notified that my dad was being transferred once again to the Great Lakes Naval Hospital near Chicago. After a period of time, my mother was finally allowed to visit my father. It was a happy ending and a new beginning for our family. Dad would eventually recover fully, but it was a tough summer for Joe and me. Both our families had experienced pain and suffering at a level that's not easy to talk about or remember.

In September of the following year (1942), my sister Jeannine was born (a true tribute to my dad's recovery)!

To me, she was a little doll who was to become the center of attention at every gathering. She was a joy for all of us and is still today. I know she loves me as much as I love her.

Life settled down quite a bit when the war ended for Joe and me. We started to go to the movies again on Saturdays. Movies in those days were double features with Roy Rogers or Gene Autry. With fifty cents in hand, we could buy a ticket, have a box of hot buttered popcorn, and still have money left to buy a comic book afterwards. Those were the days!

Starting to Grow up...

Things were changing a little for Joe and me as we started to mature a little. We played baseball in the park now instead of cowboys, and we began walking to places that we hadn't ventured out to before. Then television came along. Joe's family got the first TV on the block. After school and on Saturdays, it was over to his house to watch our favorite shows. Pretty soon, the park took a back seat to our list of activities. Suddenly (what seemed to come from nowhere), girls entered the picture.

Now Joe was bigger than me and weighed about 30 pounds more with great muscles. Girls really liked the way he looked, and boy did they pay attention to him. As for me, I was long-legged and what you would call, skinny. I was always one of the last kids to be picked for baseball games (even though I was pretty good), but Joe always came through and picked me for his team as quick as he could. What a great pal he was.

When Joe came up to bat, the guys on the field would move back because so many times he'd hit the ball so hard it would sail clear over the shelter house. In fact, Joe was so good at baseball that in his senior year in high school, the professional baseball scouts came to town to check him out. Sorry to say for Joe, nothing came of it.

Having Joe for a best friend also had other advantages. Being the skinny guy of the group, the bigger kids would sometimes try to pick on me, but Joe would step in and no one wanted to tangle with him so that would be it. He never let anyone push me around. Thank goodness for that!

Certain habits start at an early age...

I also remember that Joe started to smoke cigarettes at an early age. He'd snitch a couple of cigarettes from his dad's pack and we'd run to the park so he could smoke them. I didn't indulge in this habit at the time, but I always went with Joe when he lit up. Once in awhile, Joe's dad would whistle for him to come home because he'd see Joe smoking behind the shelter house. As soon as Joe heard that whistle, he knew he was going to get whacked and would be confined to the house for a few days.

During this punishment period, I would sneak over after school to visit with Joe. Before his dad would get home from work, I would leave. Joe's mom never said anything to me about my forbidden visits, and she certainly didn't let on to her husband either. She was a softy when it came to Joe and me.

Losing my buddy...

High school brought along even more changes for Joe and me. He met a girl in his sophomore year and she began to take up all his spare time. In a way, I became jealous, but I tried to understand. I went on my way with other friends and still hung out at the park. We started to have hot dog roasts, played games and couldn't wait for it to get dark so we could "smooch" a little with the girls who were now part of our group. My first kiss was from a girl down the block – simple clean fun (I was 12 and this was the same year I got a bicycle, a purple Monarch from Sears & Roebuck).

It was at this time that Lois came onto the scene. She was four years older than I. About sixteen as I recall now. She had a boyfriend (he was like a big ape to me). She would tell her boyfriend that I was like her little brother. I think he knew that I had a crush on his girl and teased her about her little "friend."

I thought about punching him out and stealing her away from him (boy what a dreamer I was), but of course, I never got around to trying that. Lois added many things to my life. She helped me learn how to ride my bike on the gravel paths in the park. I took a lot of spills and many cuts later, mastered the bike. Lois was there to see me do it! The next year, Lois moved away breaking my heart a little bit. Years later, I remember hearing that she got married. I wonder whatever happened to her? How did her life turn out?

With Lois gone, I really missed my buddy Joe. Oh, he would wander into the park sometimes, but most often, he would bring his girl friend along with him. I was still envious of their relationship. After all, she had come between my buddy and me!

But she didn't take up all his time as Joe and I would still meet in the park at the shelter a few times a week. Joe, and all the others who joined us, would smoke cigarettes and play cards. Those were the best of times.

What seems so funny now is a little ritual that took place for no special reason. After supper, all of us kids in the neighborhood would meet back at the park as I said before, but we'd go to the trouble of getting all spruced up, even down to changing our clothes. We would do the same thing, night after night, as if special clothes were now required when we hung out. We'd stay out until it got dark, and then home we'd go. It was an event that played out over and over. I guess it was all part of being a teenager back in my day.

Like so many around me, in my senior year, I began to smoke cigarettes like everyone else. I told my parents I wanted to try it, and they gave me the okay. It didn't seem like a big deal back then because no one really knew the dangers of smoking at that point in time. The habit was not long lived. I just never acquired a taste for cigarettes.

The gang was to break up...

Joe graduated from high school about six months ahead of me in December. As fate would have it, Joe got married right away. He didn't want to go college (most kids in the neighborhood didn't have the funds for college anyway) and most of us either went for a job right away or enlisted in the military.

Joe got a job. He and his wife lived with his parents. I remember trying to talk Joe into joining the U. S. Air Force with me, but he really wanted to stay home with his wife. At least that's what he said.

When Joe would return home from work, we would still squeeze a visit in to the park just to catch up on our different days. I would talk about school. Joe would talk about his job. Knowing Joe as well as I did, I could tell marriage and the responsibilities it brings was not all that he thought it would be. He gave me the feeling that he wished he could go into the service with me, but he just couldn't do it.

Then came the big news. I remember him saying he was trying to get a better job because there was a baby on its way! He also said that they wanted to get a place of their own.

Suddenly, I felt like I was 10 years old and Joe was 30! He was all grown up and really leaving me behind.

When my graduation from Arsenal Tech High School was final in June, I took it easy for the summer. I had some fun, saw Joe a couple of times, and then I left for the service.

By this time, I had my own steady girl, Barbara, and leaving was tougher than I thought it would be. As time advanced, I, too, got married while still serving in the Air Force and quickly became the parent of a beautiful baby boy that we named Mark. Unfortunately, we were both too young for the commitment that marriage brings and we divorced within a year.

Some three years later, I had served out my four-year military contract and was discharged. I took a few jobs until I finally decided to join the police force where I remained as a law officer for 34 years and two months to be exact. During this time period, I would remarry and have two more beautiful sons, Curt and Eric. Unfortunately, this marriage would also fail. For a time, I wasn't sure that marriage would ever be right for me.

Today, I am pleased to say that I am happily married to the love of my life and have been for over 20 years. Her name is Janet. I call her "The Redhead." We have a special, loving relationship.

When I retired from the police department, Janet and I moved to Las Vegas where we still live today. I love it here. We enjoy our life.

As for Joe, his first marriage lasted for 15 years during which time he would have two sons and a daughter. Joe would also find divorce in his future. Eventually, Joe remarried a lovely lady named, Kathy.

A few years ago, my wife and I returned to Indianapolis for the funeral of my second wife, Kay. It was a very sad day for our entire family. The next day, I called Joe and Kathy and set up a visit.

When we arrived, Kathy answered the door and said Joe was resting. She shared with us that Joe was now in very poor health and required a lot of time in bed. Shortly, though, Kathy went into the bedroom to awaken Joe and they both came down the hall together. Joe now had to use a cane, walking slowly, leaning heavily on his wife.

Janet and I were both stunned to see my old buddy, a monumental man, now down to about 125 pounds (his normal weight was somewhere around 280 pounds). Joe was short of breath, moved at a snail's gait, but had the same big, jovial smile. We exchanged hugs and sat down to chat for a while. Joe told me that he had several heart attacks followed by heart bypass surgery and a removal of a lung. For over a year, he had also been on kidney dialysis. Needless to say, each day was difficult for him.

Looking at Joe, it was so evident that poor health was taking its toll. Now, sitting in his living room, we spoke of our days in the park and life in general. We laughed a lot – even bringing tears to our eyes with some of the hilarious stories that two old buddies had shared during their lifetime.

We had not seen each other for several years due to geography and new lives separating us, so these were joyous moments together. During our conversation, I called Joe "SKINNY!" He really laughed about that and said that for a change, I was right because I finally did outweigh him.

When we left, we hugged for a lengthy time and kissed as dear friends do when parting. While Janet and I walked to the car, I said that I was afraid this would be the last time I would see Joe alive.

Still thinking about my boyhood days, we drove over to the old neighborhood and cruised past the park. The old shelter house was gone and so were several of the large trees that I remembered. Now there are many swings and slides. It had changed, just like Joe and me.

Driving past our homes, they too looked different sitting up there on a hill that didn't seem nearly as large as I remembered. I wondered out loud if the people who now lived in our old houses could ever possibly know the magic of Spade's Park and our neighborhood the way Joe and I did?

I doubt it. Ours was an experience that was unique and it will always be a part of our lives. It was a different time.

Some months ago, we received a phone call from Joe's wife, Kathy. Without her saying anything more than "It's Kathy," we knew why she had called. Yes, Joe had passed away peacefully. Kathy could barely speak she was so distraught. It was difficult to say what was in my heart, but we knew what had to be said, and we exchanged our thoughts. So many memories flashed through my mind. I knew that an important part of my life had also passed away with Joe's death. Janet and I expressed our sympathy, but as Joe would have wanted, our conversation turned to more pleasant memories of times past. Times when Joe was big and strong and living life as only he could.

When I hung up the phone, I felt a strong sense of sadness come over me. Sadness you can't talk about. You just feel it. Joe was a good friend, a special person and now he was gone. He will be missed by his old buddy.

Abiding by her husband's wishes, Kathy had Joe cremated. His ashes were spread across a beautiful pond at the cemetery. It was a private ceremony with just Kathy and his children gathered. This was how he wanted it to be.

With my dream, I have had time to reflect back on my life. I believe that in addition to family members, we all meet so many people during a lifetime. Some stay near, some move on, but maybe once (or even a few times) someone becomes as close to you as if they were a part of your own being. They are a true friend, not merely an acquaintance. They may not live next door to you or even in close proximity, but nevertheless, they become and remain an important part of your life.

This type of friendship is an essential part of who you are. This is how I felt about Joe, or as I still like to call him now, "SKINNY."

I feel as if someday, Joe and I will meet again. In my heart, I wish that we could have just one more day in the park together, the park we knew as kids.

And so I end this small remembrance with just a small portion of my childhood by wishing for my children, grandchildren and all the children of the world, a safe place to grow up with friendships to remember, and a hope that we will once again know a simpler time and a simpler life. Let's improve the future.

"Goodbye Skinny!" Thanks for sending me a great dream that brought back all those wonderful memories. Until we meet again, your buddy "Fats."

Janet and Me

Mom and Dad.
During the production of this book my mother passed
away on December 20, 2001. She was 88.

So You Want To Write A Book…

Created by:
J. Andy Murphy, author
Founder of the WriteStuff Writer's Seminars and
Getaway Trips with Ambassadair Travel Club.

For Anyone Who Has A Passion
To Learn More About Writing And Publishing!

Writing is the Silent Journey of Creation

LET'S START WITH FICTION writing as this is one of the most popular categories of publishing. First of all, what is your definition of fiction? Many people have different ideas about what constitutes a work of fiction. Fiction is a story you create from your own imagination. The story comes to life in a format that you construct based on real events or things that have never happened. Fiction can be written in several different formats: Short Stories are just that—short. They usually are within a word count range of 500 to 1,500 words. Novellas, usually have a range of 25 to 145 pages, and Novels range from 200 pages on up. You need to learn as much as you can about these three categories if you're going to work in fiction.

What is nonfiction? Simple: Nonfiction is a story that is true and based on research and/or established opinion of a subject or person. If you want to write nonfiction you will need sharp research abilities, concise construction, wonderful resources and a solid writing voice to tell your story. Sounds easy enough. Give it a whirl. Which do you like working in best: writing a story based on facts set in front of you to draw from or creating something that never existed before you thought it all up? It's your choice.

What does it take to write fiction? In my humble opinion, to write fiction takes patience, a wonderful sense of imagination and an indestructible ego. If you have answered yes to these three requirements, then read on.

J. Andy Murphy

Keep these things in mind: Fiction needs:

+ Well-Defined characters.
+ A VISUAL setting that comes to life as the story is told.
+ A good Story Concept with plots/subplots that work together.
+ Concise Time Lines.
+ A well constructed Set Up for story/characters to work through.
+ A Champion(s). (Characters who take the leading part in a story/novel.)
+ Bad Guy(s). (Characters that oppose another; an adversary.)
+ A Solid conclusion.
+ A good TITLE.

What kept you from writing today?

_____

_____

_____

_____

_____

_____

_____

_____

Developing Strong Characters

WHAT BRINGS A READER into a story and then keeps them turning the pages? Usually, it is well-defined character(s) that the reader can IDENTIFY with, BOND with, and more than anything else, ROOT on to a good outcome. And let's not forget to add a plot that is intriguing and well paced.

As you start creating keep in mind the following:

+ A writer needs to be able to describe the physical side of the character(s).
+ A writer doesn't have to give a two-page description of what this person(s) looks like, but you do have to make them visible to the reader.
+ Give characters (good and bad) faults, warts and personal challenges.
+ Give the protagonist a compassionate/difficult side that surfaces little by little as the reader gets into the story.
+ Be careful with the names you pick for your characters.
+ Gradually unfold what makes them (characters) tick, what hardships they've had to overcome in life, what they want out of life. Why are they rotten to the core? Stronger than steel. Void of emotion. Let the reader see inside the character a little bit to better understand their actions.
+ Give the reader a background profile on your characters.

+ Introduce your character(s) with a set up. Take them forward to a challenge.
+ Bring their story to a conclusion.
+ Create a character by observing people that you find interesting in looks and manner.
+ When your characters engage in conversation, make the dialogue real and natural. Try using italic for all dialogue in your draft as this really helps you to hear the words that you've written. Try reading the dialogue out loud as well.
+ Give your main character an opportunity for another novel. In other words, don't kill them off at the end of the story unless you absolutely have no other choice. Think book series!
+ Only create a character if they have something relevant to bring to the storyline.
+ Too many characters can ruin a novel. Readers can't keep track of who's who.
+ Above all else, make your characters come to life with your words.
+ Don't write an epic. Be concern with the length of your story. It's important.

What kept you from writing today?

_____

_____

_____

_____

_____

_____

_____

_____

Learn to Write with Fewer Words

MOST WRITERS SHARE one common problem. The gift of gab! As writers, we think every word we place on white paper is necessary. In reality, as you grow, you will learn to use less words, but in a more powerful and effective way.

Learning to condense and control your writing pattern is not easy. A good editor will usually do it for you as most editors are taught to keep only what's good and what's actually needed to get the point across to the reader. What do I mean by "writing tight?" Examine the flow of the following three writing examples.

Examples of condensing descriptive sentences:

Long version: (4 sentences)

"The room appeared to be cramped and poorly cared for at first glance. There were pieces of Ryan's life scattered about in an ill cared for manner—a picture here, a piece of clothing there. The lights were dim creating a slightly dark atmosphere that made you uncomfortable and just a bit unsettled. How could this be all that's left of a man, who for all appearances had it all?"

Tighter version: (3 sentences)

"The room was unkempt, dark and unsettling. Ryan's personal effects were scattered about the room in a careless manner. Was this to be all that's left of a man, who for all appearances had it all?"

Really condensed version: (1 sentence)
"Ryan's presence and all that he appeared to be was nowhere to be found in this dismal room."

This is an exercise I found in a good book some time ago that helped me to work my way into tighter writing. It shows how a writer could vary a descriptive style. Keep in mind there are times when a flowery narrative is important. But more times than not, tighter writing is needed. Make it a habit to ask this question: Is it all really needed? Could I get the point across with fewer, but stronger words? If the answer is no—then go for the epic! Remember, it's your novel and you have to live with it in the end. Writing should be fun and fulfilling. If it isn't, well maybe you are writing for all the wrong reasons.

What kept you from writing today?

_____

_____

_____

_____

_____

_____

_____

_____

Four Rules of Mystery

A LARGE PART OF fiction writing today falls in the category of mystery. Taking a cue from the leading mystery writers, the following rules seem to apply:

+ A writer must create a crime with impact.
  Readers must care about the plot(s) in order to finish reading the story.
+ Give an early introduction to the villain.
  You don't need to quickly identify he/she as the bad guy, but don't wait until final chapter to bring him/her/them into the story.
+ Create a likeable protagonist.
  You want your readers to root/identify with this character.
+ Give enough, but not too many clues.
  Don't make the crime so easy to solve that you insult the reader's intelligence.

There! That seems simple enough. Now try writing a short story composed of 500 words or less using these rules. If you nail it, you're on your way to creating a good novel.

J. Andy Murphy

What kept you from writing today?

_____

_____

_____

_____

_____

_____

_____

_____

Twenty Golden Rules for Writing as Suggested by the Pros:

+ Learn to write in a concise manner.
+ Don't be afraid to trim your sentences.
+ Describe tightly.
+ Get to the point. Make it a sentence, not a rambling paragraph.
+ Read each paragraph out loud. How does it sound? Can you say it with less?
+ Make every word count.
+ Make every character count.
+ Write in a "speaking tone."
+ Visualize each and every sentence. Does it all flow?
+ Find you own voice.
+ Be comfortable with your own style of writing.
+ Become an observer of people, places and things.
+ Keep index cards with people descriptions that you've observe while out.
+ Use color when describing a person. Bring them to life in the reader's mind as you introduce them.
+ Understand how important good research is in the writing process.
+ Find a way to make writing work for you in your own time and space.
+ Don't use excuses to keep you away from your writing time.

+ Develop an outline, or scene cards to help you develop your story and keep it on track.
+ Write with passion.
+ WRITE EVERY BLASTED DAY!

What kept you from writing today?

_____

_____

_____

_____

_____

_____

_____

Getting Organized to Write

+ Find your personal comfort zone! Every writer needs to find their own comfort zone for writing. What works for one may not work for another. Writing can be as simple as sitting down with a large yellow pad and jotting down your story in pencil. This is the way some of the best novels were first created. But as time progressed, we were blessed with the development of personal computers. Another method is to use a voice recorder. Talk your story out and then convert to the written word. You'd be surprised how well this simple method works. Whichever format fits your personal style of creation best should be used.
+ Don't make it all too complicated. Rituals are just that—rituals.
+ Define your work and your audience—in other words: Know your Genre!
+ So what is Genre? Genre is a class or category of artistic endeavor having a particular form, content, technique, or the like.

Bookstores will place your book in a certain section according to the genre category that it is written in: fiction, nonfiction, history, cookbooks, mysteries, romance, self-help and travel are a few of these genres. It is important to know what genre your book falls into so that a publisher clearly knows how to place it within their own catalog of information.

What type of book are you trying to write?

+ A Thriller
+ A Children's Story – children under five; young reader; young adult; teen, picture book. There are many age levels to consider when writing for children
+ Biography
+ True Crime
+ Historical Biography
+ Memoirs
+ How-to Book/Self-Help
+ Historical Fiction
+ Western
+ Romance – adult or teen
+ Science Fiction
+ Other

Make sure you have a clear understanding of the kind of book you are creating. This is your artistic endeavor and like all things in life, you must be able to clearly identify where it fits.

A few tips that help in the organizational process:

+ Establish a timetable for writing everyday.
+ Put writing on your daily schedule.
+ Research your subject (fiction/nonfiction) BEFORE you begin to write.
+ Give yourself a start and an ending date.
+ Seek out a good book editor to look at your work before you move on to creating a book proposal.
+ Have a clear idea of why you need to create a solid "book proposal" document. You can't sell your book to a publisher with words alone. You must have this very important element in place.

The most important advice ever given to a writer is that which is founded in the discipline of the profession. Every writer needs to FIT writing into their daily lives. It shouldn't feel like drudgery, but should be looked at as a time to create and spin off all those creative juices that you have as a writer. Make a commitment to yourself to complete your work. A writer must also learn to "LET GO" of the work. One of the biggest problems facing publishers today is getting the work in on time. Publishers work on tight deadlines and nothing will kill an acceptance contract faster than a delay from the writer.

Writing does require a COMMITMENT of one's time. A good writer is organized, and through that organization finds the time to put their own words down on paper and the result of this effort is a finished book! Isn't that worth the journey?

What kept you from writing today?

_____

_____

_____

_____

_____

_____

_____

_____

How to Build a Novel Proposal

FIRST YOU WRITE THE STORY. If you think that's the hard part of your writing experience you may be in for a surprise if you want to take it to the next level: getting it published. There are several factors you must understand for the second part of your journey called writing a book proposal. How hard is this you ask? It's so important you may want to invest in a whole book devoted to just this process. I can suggest How To Write A Book Proposal by: Michael Larsen, AAR – Revised Edition. It really guides you through this process. In the meantime, to help you understand it just a little bit, I've created a short overview of this process. Just simple steps that cover the basic rules of creating book proposals.

Just the basics

- Writer must create a very good Query or Cover letter.
- A good synopsis is critical.
- Be prepared to include at least three consecutive sample chapters.
- Furnish a chapter-by-chapter outline.
- Provide/develop an author biography.
- Consider securing endorsements from knowledgeable individuals for your story/work if it's nonfiction.

What is a Query letter?

A query letter is your letter of inquiry or introduction for your work. It serves two functions: to communicate to an agent or editor/ publisher what you have to offer, and to ask if there is interested in seeing it.

All good queries contain:

+ A grabber or hook leading sentence that makes the reader/editor/publisher want to get his/her hands on actual novel.
+ One to three paragraphs about your novel.
+ A short paragraph about you and your publishing credentials if you have any.
+ A good reason why you're contacting this agent/publisher instead of another.
+ The length of the intended novel.
+ A sentence or two about the intended audience.
+ A SASE (self-addressed, stamped envelope).
+ A Marketing Plan.

One other important element to share with you is to always send copies of your manuscript when requested. Never send your one and only master copy.

DOs and DON'Ts that might make a difference:

+ Do state any writing credits that you have earned.
+ Do state if your novel isn't finished, and give the date your manuscript will be completed.
+ Be upfront about simultaneous submissions to other agents and editors.
+ Do address your letter to a specific agent or editor.
+ Don't be afraid to mention that you've never been published.

+ Don't spend much time trying to sell yourself. Your work should do that.
+ Don't state that some other agent or publisher has rejected your novel.
+ Don't ask for advice or criticism.
+ Do summarize any relevant experience you have in writing.
+ Don't mention anything about yourself not pertinent to the novel.
+ Don't bring up payment (advance/royalty) expectations.
+ Don't mention copyright information.
+ Don't staple your query letter to your manuscript.
+ Try and keep all this under two pages.

Other dos and don'ts.

+ Do thank the editor/agent for their consideration and time.
+ Do give the novel's exact word count.
+ Don't include your social security number or other personal information.
+ Don't put a page number on the query letter.

Cover Page

This is exactly the same as the cover page you'll use with the ultimate manuscript. It includes the title, an estimated word count and either your name and address or your agent's name and address (if you're submitting through an agent) and contact number.

+ Don't include both of the above. Use one or another depending on the situation.
+ Don't use a header or number on the title page.

Table of contents

This should let the editor/publisher know precisely what's in your book proposal package. You need to include a slugline in the top left margin. It should contain:

+ Your last name, a slash, your novel's title in all capital letters, another slash, and the word Contents.
+ It should look like this: Murphy/THE TIME DIAL/ Contents.
+ Drop down about six lines and put the heading "Proposal Contents" or "Contents" flush with the left margin in bold large font.
+ Then list all the contents. Be sure to catalog every item you're sending in your proposal and the corresponding page numbers as they appear in your proposal.
+ Make your contents page easy to read, which means organizing it according to sections and double-spacing. Do not number the page.

Synopsis

The synopsis supplies key information about your novel (plot, theme, characterization, setting), while also showing how all these go together to form the big picture for your story. You want to give a clear picture of your proposed book without making the editor or agent read the entire novel.

+ There is no exact rule for how many pages a synopsis should be.
+ Most publishers seem to prefer a short synopsis that runs from one to two single-spaced pages, or three to five double-spaced pages.
+ Some plot-heavy fiction, such as thrillers and mysteries, might need more space and can run from 10 to 25 double-spaced pages, depending on the length of the manuscript and the number of plot shifts.

✦ If you must use a longer synopsis, aim for one synopsis page to every 25 pages (a 250 page manuscript should get a 10-page synopsis). Try to keep it as short as you can.

✦ Your synopsis should have a beginning, a middle and an ending (yes, you must tell how the novels ends). The publisher needs to know this information to round out your synopsis correctly.

An Outline

An outline is often used interchangeably with a synopsis. *There is a difference.* While a synopsis is a brief, encapsulated version of the novel at large, an outline makes each chapter its own story, usually containing a few paragraphs per chapter. Try to keep each chapter to about a page, and begin each chapter on a different page.

✦ Never submit an outline unless an agent or editor specifically asks for it.

✦ Outlines most often are requested by genre fiction editors, because genre books run for many pages and have numerous plot shifts.

Endorsements page

(Usually not needed when writing fiction.)

An endorsement page — it's not written in stone, but it helps to have one attached if it's a nonfiction story. For instances, if you are writing a story about heart disease, it would help to have an endorsement for your story information coming from a leading heart surgeon.

What is an endorsement page? It is a list of quotes concerning your work/novel. The hard part comes in getting noteworthy people, typically prominent industry insiders (well-known authors, agents, editors, experts on the topic) who have read your work and like it enough to comment favorably on it.

49

+ Don't use your husband, wife, family, neighbors or writing group quotes. This kind of quote won't help your book.
+ It's best not to include an endorsement page unless you have at least two good quotes from well-known, well-respected sources.
+ Don't fret if you don't have any endorsements.

Few authors include one with fiction manuscripts (unless you have a personal letter from Tom Clancy telling you how he envies your writing style).

Novel manuscript

Your novel manuscript is easy to format and submit. What's most important is that you know when and what to submit. For instance:

+ Never send an entire manuscript until you've been requested to do so. It is a waste of time and money.
+ Check the agent's/publisher requirements to see if he or she even accepts unsolicited manuscripts. (Check this out in the Writer's Market Guide, available in most bookstores/libraries.)
+ Your entire package/presentation must be letter perfect with NO mistakes.
+ Proof everything you've written at least five times.
+ Hire an editor to make sure it's word-perfect in grammar and spelling.
+ Don't trust a Spell Checker to find all your mistakes!
+ First impressions are many times your ONLY impression.

A Marketing Plan

This is the part of becoming an author that most writers never think about. In today's difficult world of publishing, a writer needs to keep in mind the business side of this market.

A writer should look beyond what the "publisher" is going to do for them and think about what "they" can do to help this book be a sales success. YES! You must be able to talk about your book with the idea of making a sale.

Every prospective author should look in their own backyard for sales opportunities. How many sales are available close to home? How much can you make happen? What are your resources on the local scene? You need to outline this information to your desired publisher. You can't be shy about the selling side of writing a book. You also can't expect a publisher to include this in their agenda. Many publishers today on the national scene offer little marketing support once a book is spawned. Many do not even pick up the author's book tour expenses. This also goes without saying that many publishers do not arrange book tours.

The following suggestions might help in understanding the marketing process and what a writer can do to assist his/her publisher.

A few things a writer can do to help promote the sale of their own book:

+ Create personal public speaking opportunities.
+ Contact regional libraries and ask to be included in writing events.
+ Discover out-of-the-box sites to host book signings: grocery stores, churches, schools, alumni events, synagogues, restaurants, specialty stores, retirement homes, etc. If it's open to the public, you'll want to talk to them!
+ Write press releases to local and regional newspapers and ask for coverage/review.
+ Contact local radio/television affiliates with talk show formats and ask to be a guest.
+ Create a mailing list of all family, friends and associates with intention to send out notification when they can support you at local bookstores.

+ Hire your own publicity firm to help market your book.
+ Remember that you are only limited by your own imagiation.
+ Remember that sales are the name of the game in the publishing world.

These are just a few things that an author can do to help promote their work. Keep in mind that national publishing houses are taking on very few new writers. A marketing plan that speaks to all the things you can do to help them promote your book is an added plus in your approach.

This is especially important if you do not have the services of an agent/publicist. It shows the publisher that you are aware of all that needs to be done to help promote your book with a successful sales outcome and that you are willing to go the extra mile to accomplish. Many local writers that were lucky enough to publish nationally found out the hard way that marketing support was not forthcoming in their national publishing experience. If a marketing plan and who is going to do what is not clearly included in your publishing contract, you may find yourself on the short end of marketing/publicity support.

The results can determine if a second book gets picked up. On the national level book sales in the 12,000 to 14,000 range are considered "dismal." This attitude stands even if the publisher did little to help circulate their own property. On a regional level, without marketing support, the average writer sells below two thousand copies. So keep your day job as there's not a lot of money in publishing at this sales level.

If you want to add that extra pitch, then do include a solid marketing plan in your query letter. It can make a difference in how a publisher looks at you as a writing partner.

Summary

The process of submitting your work to a publisher/agent is not easy. More than likely, you will be rejected on the first (maybe 50) tries. But if your desire to publish is sincere, there will be a way to realize your dream. My three golden rules for survival are:

+ Be passionate and professional about your work!
+ Believe in yourself!
+ Be realistic!

What kept you from writing today?

_____

_____

_____

_____

_____

_____

_____

To the Web We Will Go!

THE FOLLOWING WEBSITES may be helpful in tracking down marketing information. They can also help in keeping you current in news about the publishing industry.

www.amazon.com

Books — This is the one of the oldest and biggest on-line bookstores. This site will also help you to discover what's all ready in print and what subjects are being covered by other writers.

www.barnesandnoble.com

Barnes & Noble — this is your local bookseller. It's like going to the store without ever leaving your easy chair. Barnes & Noble have many bookstores spread across the United States.

www.bookbrowse.com

BookBrowse.com offers excellent excerpts of bestsellers and much, much more. A fun site.

www.ingrambook.com

Ingram's is one of several major book distributors in the United States and Canada. Ingrams is involved in the very important distribution system that lands your book in the mainstream arm of bookstores. Bookstore managers, customer relations reps, etc. will turn to Ingram to order your book. Partners and Baker & Taylor are other leading book distributors. If you decide to "Self-Publish" you need to understand the relationship between bookstores and such distributors. You can't get your book in most cases into a local bookstore without a contract in place with one of these BIG FELLAS.

www.nyt.com

This is the New York Times on the Internet. You can look at their top thirty-bestseller lists and gauge the popularity of your book subject matter.

www.bookwire.com

This is R.R.Bowker's BookWire site. This site deals mostly with subscription, but you can retrieve some basic information for free, and it has pathways to other AAR agent's sites, Publishers Weekly, and many more.

www.bookwire.com/pw/pw.html

Publisher's Weekly home page site. An excellent site to become familiar with in your publishing journey.

www.uop.edu/misc/bookpub.html

This site offers the name of Book Publishers on the Web

www.writersdigest.com

This national distributed magazine site should serve as your first source for information on creative writing, competitions and contests, courses and so much more.

What kept you from writing today?

_____

_____

_____

_____

_____

_____

_____

_____

Other forms of publishing

ELECTRONIC PUBLISHING is using an Internet provider as your publisher. Plain and simple, it is a way to have your work published other than the traditional form. You will pay for the production of your work. It is a type of self-publishing and the costs are considerably less than some forms of vanity publishing.

There are several different types of electronic publishing. For instance, electronic publishing, or e-publishing, produces and stores books electronically. E-books are distributed in a variety of ways such as on-line, on disk, or on CD-ROM or DVD, usually as a file or series of files. These files can be downloaded directly to a handheld electronic device.

Print-on-Demand (POD) publishing has risen from an afterthought to a very viable way to realize your dream of publishing. POD houses all offer formats that will assist you with publishing your work. You will be paying for these services and should make yourself knowledgeable about all the different services available with each POD publisher. You will need to have some computer skills to transmit your work or can rely on a computer technician to help you. Most POD houses are very user friendly in the technical end and will work with you to make this a seamless project. Like any other process, do your homework and learn about the company you want to serve as your publishing partner.

POD publishers will host your book on their site and a reader can order directly. POD publishers also have unique formulas for the royalty process. Don't be shy in asking about this feature when you are considering publishing. The author usually receives a small number of printed books when the project is completed. The author can order more books and will pay a reduced fee for his own personal orders. Usually, there is no royalty attached when an author orders books for their own personal stock. Check this beforehand so you will have a clear understanding of your process.

Once a book has been ordered by a reader, the shipment varies between 48-hours and 10-working days as a rule. Royalty fees are a bit higher to the author than the traditional publishing experience, but there is no such thing as advances. You will receive a quarterly copy of your sales with a check. The process is similar to traditional houses: you submit your work on disk with hard copy. You will pay for each selected service above the standard format (extra editing, cover design, marketing services, etc.). Your book will be listed on www. amazon.com and will appear in their personal Internet site. Reviews can be posted and other such services will apply.

Like any other selection process, if you decide to publish through an Internet source, there are a few questions to ask:

+ Does the publisher have a good Web site?
+ Do you like how they post their other books on the site?
+ Will they furnish you with an ISBN number?
+ Who is their distribution source? Ingrams? Partners?
+ Baker & Taylor?
+ What is their policy on booksignings? Do they accept returns from bookstores?
+ Can they place your book in a bookstore?
+ Have they won awards or praise from worthwhile organizations?
+ Is the publisher asking for money up front?
+ If so, be on your guard.
+ Who have they published? What do they consider a sales success to be?

+ Does the publisher use a proprietary format, or do they port the book to different formats such as Internet download using Acrobat's PDF format, print-on-demand, RocketBooks, or Palm Pilot? Do they offer only downloads or disks as well?
+ Does the publisher get reviews for their author's books? If so, where?
+ Do they advertise in places where bookstore buyers, libraries, schools and other market ordering sources will see your book?
+ What is their marketing plan for your book? What do they charge for this service?
+ What are their costs for editing, design? Compare these costs to securing your own book editor or illustrator or pagination specialist.
+ What services do they offer to help you publicize your book and at what price?
+ Will they furnish you a finished copy of one of their produced books for your personal review?

The key in any self-publishing journey is to not be afraid to ask questions. Also, you need to decide in advance how much money you are willing to spend to see your work in print? Internet (POD) publishers such as Author House, IUniverse, Infinity and Trafford offer an array of self-publishing menu services. Review these charges carefully and select what best fits your budget.

Keep one thing in mind; traditional publishers are few and far between. Regional publishers have limited budgets and university presses usually want only a limited category of work. To interest a national publisher is a very difficult journey and will usually involve a contract with a literary agent. The publishing journey isn't easy and it's getting much harder as we speak. It takes a lot of money to get a book in print. Publishers are on tight budgets and they accept only the cream of the crop. More than any other reason, this is why the format of Internet publishing is coming into its own age.

What kept you from writing today?

_____

_____

_____

_____

_____

_____

_____

The following are a few ways to help you develop ideas for stories, whether fiction on nonfiction:

+ Read — read all kinds of newspapers and magazines. This will supply you with current and timely topics.
+ Become a people watcher. Play a game where you imagine what their life is really about?
+ Try creating a new life for them. See where it all goes.
+ Look back on something that happened to you or someone you know. Change the outcome of these events?
+ Practice writing an opening "hook" or sentence that will start your story.
+ Rewrite Snow White or Robin Hood. Create a new storyline for these classics. Or create a new gender for an old story character.
+ Go to trade shows and find out what's hot in the industry, any industry.
+ Spend time in your local bookstores and always visit a new bookstore when you travel.
+ TIVO old movies that are playing on your cable stations. Look at the plots. Could you do better?
+ Research your own family for its history and interesting stories.
+ Keep a little notebook with notes of interesting places and people that you meet. Don't leave home without it!
+ Ask your friends to tell you about their family stories. There's gold to be found in listening.

J. Andy Murphy

What kept you from writing today?

_____

_____

_____

_____

_____

_____

_____

_____

Did You Know

+ A book of fiction is also called a novel. Only amateurs use the term fiction novel, which is a redundancy.
+ Nonfiction describes a book that narrates actual events or information and opinion. It embraces all other types of books other than fiction.
+ A genre is a marketing term that divides and categorizes books so that they are easily placed together in a store. Westerns, romances, and mysteries are examples of genres.
+ A series is made up of two or more books linked by the same character, the same "world" within the books, or a brand name.
+ The word bestseller usually refers to a book that appears on a top 10 or top 15 list of best-selling books. The three major lists are compiled by the New York Times, the industry magazine Publishers Weekly, and USA Today.
+ A parody is a humorous imitation of a famous work.
+ A book that's in print is still available from the publisher.
+ A book that's out of print is no longer available from the publisher
+ A list is a publishing house term for the books it is currently publishing or intending to publish. Backlists are lists of books already published. Frontlists are a list of books about to be published or currently published.
+ Authors are subject to the dreaded "return" process. This means that the books that were ordered for a signing or for general sales didn't make the cut during the 30 days

or so that typically applies to "bookshelf" space and are being sent back. These books will be "back charged" by a publisher and will cut into royalty fees. Also, the books do not always come back in the best of shape and are subject to lost sales. In a nutshell: Just because a bookstore ordered 30 of your books doesn't guarantee that all will be sold. Average bookstore order could consist of five books. Be grateful for any order!

+ A book that is remaindered is sold at a deep discount in a store prior to the book going out of print.

What kept you from writing today?

_____
_____
_____
_____
_____
_____
_____
_____

Should I Copyright Material That I Create?

TECHNICALLY, YOUR WORK IS copyrighted the second you create it! Writers sometimes mail a copy of their manuscript to themselves and keep the envelope unopened to prove that the work existed on the day of the postmark.

If you want to register your work with the U.S. Copyright Office go to www.copyright.gov or mail a request to the Copyright Office, Library of Congress, 101 Independence Avenue, S. E., Washington, D.C. 20559-6000. The fee is $30 per registration. You can get more information by calling the hotline: 202-707-9100.

Remember, you can only copyright the way you express an idea, not the idea itself.

A Few Cliff Notes for Publishing

"What great thing would you attempt if you knew you could not fail?"

— Dr. Robert H. Schuller

Interesting fact: If you put 100 people in a room, 10 will tell you that they are writing a book. Out of those 10, only one will seriously devote the time and effort to even start an outline. Books don't get published without a giant effort on behalf of the writer. But the journey is certainly worth the effort!

A few words of wisdom from one writer to another...

+ Read as much as you can.
+ Enroll in good writing courses.
+ Never think you know it all!
+ Write something everyday.
+ Learn when you are most creative—10 minutes of good writing is far better than eight hours of bad writing.
+ Be selfish with your writing time.
+ Develop your own voice or writing style.
+ Develop an outline format to help keep you on track.
+ Learn how to bring a character or scene to life through description (especially important in fiction writing).

+ Keep track of your story's time-line. Years, seasons, locations and dates need to flow correctly as story ages/progresses.
+ Keep the passion in your treatment overview (A treatment is a detailed, but short synopsis of your story idea).
+ Create "index file card systems" where you can retain interesting future story ideas.
+ Become a "smart editor" for your own work: Write it-Read it-Tighten it up!
+ Don't be afraid of creating several "Chapter Drafts." Find the one that really works and then move on.
+ Don't create a War and Peace epic. Keep an eye on the length of your story. It is important. If it's more than 300 pages, consider a serial process.
+ If you're serious about writing, invest in good computer equipment (large screen, good memory bank and a decent printer). It pays for itself in the end.
+ Come to terms with the "loneliness of writing." It is a journey that requires dedication.
+ Expect to suffer moments of "blocked creativity." Every cure is different.
+ Understand that it may be a simple fact of loss of confidence.
+ Believe in yourself. "For every dark night, there is a rising sun."

"Life is about turning the things you really want to do into the things you've done."

— Smart Start

What kept you from writing today?

_____

_____

_____

_____

_____

_____

_____

_____

When you're ready to seek out a publisher you should:

+ Learn the correct formats for submission per publisher. They all vary.
+ Buy a copy of the latest version of Writer's Digest "The Writer's Market." Or check out a copy from your nearest library. A world of publishing information can be found in this one resource.
+ Before you forward your work to a publisher, make sure the name of the person you have secured is still in place.
+ Make sure you have their correct title and current address.
+ Don't be afraid to call for this information.
+ If you can make a brief contact beforehand, do so, but don't overstay your welcome. Editors don't have time to listen to your entire story at this point.
+ Learn how to write a good query letter that includes a "marketing support" feature.
+ Identify what you can do to help in the sale of your book (consider hiring a local publicity agent or make contact with a promotions specialist company).
+ Be candid in your ability to tackle public speaking. If you can handle it, include a list of possible events for your book to be offered for sale.
+ Include any information you can on your region's library support for book signing possibilities.

+ Present your manuscript in a professional format. Don't go to any great expense to accomplish this, just submit with plain 60-pound cover page and back page. Secured manuscript with plated brass fasteners in a two or three ring format. (I.5 or 2 inch is the best fit for most manuscripts.)
+ Don't rely on "spell-check" to catch all the spelling/grammar errors.
+ Don't rely on friends to check your work. Get in contact with a good editor.
+ Know your market when searching for a publisher.
+ Learn about regional publishers and their niche in the marketplace.
+ Know that Internet publishers may have different requirements for submission than traditional publishers.
+ Understand the ramification of "multiple submissions."
+ Keep track of all submissions for follow-up. It's okay to call after a few days to make sure they have received your work. It's not okay to call once a week to find out if they might want to publish it.
+ Understand what a publisher will mean to you. Publishers underwrite the cost of printing, distribution, audit checks, managing receipts writing large checks for services you know nothing about. Here are a few thoughts for you to digest as you start this process of self-publishing:
+ Define the reach and the audience that might be interested in your story. In other words are there more than a handful of people out there who might be interested in your story? If not, then only print a few copies or consider emailing your story to those who have an interest.
+ When the audience is identified, do a marketing/business plan that will set the stage for delivering your book to the public.
+ Know the market and fair printing prices if you decide to self-publish.
+ Don't be afraid to ask for comparison printing quotes here and abroad.

+ Establish a set "galley preview/author sign off" sheet at each step of the printing process.
+ Investigate graphic support through free-lancer artists for jacket/cover design.
+ Take an active part in the pagination (page layout) process of your book.
+ Invest in good Back Cover copy and Jacket Flap copy for hardcover titles. Keep it simple. Remember it's a selling point to the reader. Work hard on this as a reader will many times decide to buy a book based on what they read in these spaces.
+ Invest in a good "fine-line editor."
+ Understand the need to send information in the correct form to Trade Announcement Listings, Book Clubs, Publisher's Weekly and other such sources.
+ Learn the negotiating process for the business side of your book. What can you expect? What is fair market?
+ Create a good "media kit" that contains pertinent information on your book including: author photo, colored copy of book front, ordering process, publisher, ISBN (International Standard Book Number) codes and a current bio. Include a brief overview of the book if you do not intend to include a copy of your book in the kit. The media kit is nothing more than a standard Oxford folder with pockets. Usually, a colored photo of the cover of your book is pasted on the folder front. You can go fancier, but it all costs money. Above all, your media kit should be complete and look professional.
+ If your story has a national audience, consider securing a national media list or other such directories.
+ Learn to write good "press releases." Make sure you always include phone number(s) for follow-up/additional questions/ interview opportunities for the media to react. You might want to follow the Who/What/Where/When/Why format of construction for your press releases.
+ Correctly identify the media officials (and their preferred method of contact) that you will need to approach for coverage on your book.

+ Don't call an "Editorial Editor" in regard to a Book Review or Feature Story. That's not their turf! Know the format and special sections of the newspaper you are sending your press release or book to for review or feature consideration. A large number of local newspapers no longer have a book editor on staff. Check out the feature sections and call to ask an editor where you should direct your information to in each case if you do not have a confirmed source. It takes a bit of leg work to get all of this in order, but it can mean the difference of getting some attention for your book or ending up in an editor's wastebasket.

+ Again, check to see if the paper has a "Book Editor or Features Editor." Direct your release there. Call first to make sure you are headed in the proper direction. The media is usually pretty good in this area of helpfulness.

+ Understand the need for connecting contracts to distribution houses such as Partners, Ingram, Baker & Taylor or Atlas. Call them up and ask what you need to do to get into the bookstores they serve. Go to their Websites and investigate the options available.

+ Spend time learning the system of ISBN (International Standard Book Number) codes needed for publishing and the importance of having a bar code on the back cover of your book if you want to sell your book to retail outlets such as bookstores. Also be aware there are different kinds of bar codes depending on the market (commercial/bookstores). These codes can change and you will need to update your information. Call your local bookstore and ask a book buyer what ISBN bar code system they are currently using.

+ Be aware of how to go about securing an ISBN number on your own? You don't just buy one ISBN. They are sold in batches (10 or so) and the price is around $250.00. Go to: info@bowker.com and investigate all the ends and outs of obtaining your own ISBN system.

+ Protect your work! Invest in registering your story idea. Writer's Guild of America West requires $20.00 per submission. Forward completed manuscript/outline/title and your name, address, social security number to: Writer's Guild of America West, 7000 West 3rd Street, Los Angeles, CA 90048 – ATTENTION: Registration. You can call WGAW at: (323) 951-4000 for any additional information. Things change so keep current.

+ In the back of your book, you might want to think about adding a page for ordering additional books or a direct number where the reader can purchase additional copies or a Website address if you have one.

+ If you intend to be selling direct to the public, you will need to investigate your own ability to accept charge cards. Go to your local banker and have this personal vendor discussion. Consider contracting with Pay Pal. Pay Pal is on the Web and they clearly outline what you have to do to set up this charge card process with them.

+ Create your own business plan with a budget to handle all the costs of producing, marketing, storing and shipping. Self-publishing comes with multiple out-of-pocket expenses. You can go broke in this process if you're not business savvy.

+ Last but not least, Never stop believing in yourself. If there is a will, there is a way.

What kept you from writing today?

_____

_____

_____

_____

_____

_____

_____

_____

Questions You Should Ask

Q: Do I need an agent?

A: It all depends on a writer's resolve to tackle a very narrow publishing industry. In most cases, an agent can help you get past all the red tape involved in selecting and reaching a publisher. Remember one thing: Agents are not easy to get. Writers outnumber them many times over.

Q: What does an agent do?

A: Agents are not all alike. Some do more than others for you. An agent can help you make it through to a waiting publisher. They will handle the negotiations concerning your rights and your royalties. Another role they can serve is to help you evaluate your work with a critical eye. An agent is in personal contact with publishers and they are aware of the criteria each one requires. In some cases, an agent can also help in the marketing of your book to bookstores and other sites. They can establish a signing calendar and make all the advance calls to their bookstores contacts. Is an agent absolutely necessary? No, but it sure helps to have a good one working for you. If a writer feels they have a book with a national interest draw, an agent is then an added, and in most cases, needed tool in breaking the barriers into publishing. Many national publishers will not work with writers not contracted to an agent. Look to The Writer's Market guidebook to help you better understand this process.

Q: What does an agent charge?

A: They usually expect a 15% cut of a writer's royalties across the board on books, films rights, and anything else they can negotiate for their client. They SHOULD NEVER ask for a monthly service fee or a reading fee. They DO have the right to charge you for postage, telephone calls and other items of expense that they occur in the approach process. Usually this amount is limited to $300.00. Make sure you know what they expect to be paid for before you sign any contract.

Q: What if they ask for money upfront to help you?

A: Call another agent!

What kept you from writing today?

_____

_____

_____

_____

_____

_____

_____

_____

Other Questions to Consider

Q: Does self-publishing always require a strong effort in personal marketing?

A: Yes, if you have any intention of selling the book to the public. If you have no experience in this check out the book "Jump start Your Book Sales" by Marilyn & Tom Ross. Lots of good information.

Q: Do you know how to price a book for sale purposes?

A: My simple rule: You need to pay the cost of the printing/storing/shipping/marketing and still come in at a fair market price for the size of your book. Paperbacks range in the $3.95 to $15.95 category. Try to keep your book under $20.00 if at all possible. Don't underprice—Don't overprice!

Q: Do you know how important a good book cover design is?

A: This is an important element for your book. A good book cover rates in the top three areas that draw in perspective buyers.

ADDITIONAL SOURCES TO REMEMBER:

The Writer's Market–Guide to publishers, agents, submission process, e-mail addresses, etc.

What kept you from writing today?

_____

_____

_____

_____

_____

_____

_____

_____

My brother's story was based on true events in his life. This story is an example of short fiction. I try to write short stories like this on a regular basis to keep my writing rhythm in place. It is an exercise that allows me to create a story from something that is in fact based on truth. It also stimulates my abilities to create dialogue. I enjoyed writing this story. And that, my friends, is what writing is all about!

An example of short fiction...

The Take-Away's

The Oval Office was crammed with the regular A-list Cabinet and Senate movers and shakers all talking at once trying to make their point to the man in charge. The blank look on his face, though, did little to reassure those assembled that he was absorbing the key issues of the message they wanted him to deliver to the nation in less than three hours. Harry Cornett, Chief of Staff, seeing that all too familiar expression on the President's face, decided to react.

"Okay gentlemen. I think we've worked this as much as we can. The President needs the room."

Like bees going after honey, the room cleared leaving the President alone with his closest friend. Cornett let the silence embrace his boss for several moments, watching the President's body language to see how quickly he was going to be able to bring up the subject that he had been avoiding all day long.

His friend of nearly 30-years, James R. Grissam, had been elected President of the United States with overwhelming numbers. He had run a flawless campaign under a democratic flag that made virtually no mistakes. He had everything the public demanded of a presidential candidate; looks, charisma, as well as a campaign message the nation wanted to hear at that moment in time — economic stability, and the big one — the one that put him over the top; to back America out of war on all foreign shores. The timing was right for such a bold statement as the Mideast had proven to be another Vietnam for our military and America was tired of fighting for a race of people who gained more pleasure from suffering and death than they did from living. No matter how many dictators were eradicated in those desert lands, another one always rose from the ashes.

So tonight President Grissam would give his second State of the Union address from a script that read nothing like the one being passed out to the media beforehand.

"Mr. President, I think we need to go over this agenda one more time."

"Harry. There's nothing left to talk about," Grissam answered roughly. Corbett looked away knowing the President was not about to change his mind.

President Grissam turned his chair to face the large oval window that looked out into the garden. Strong emotions painfully registered in his face.

"It's time for America to do what it should have done 20 years ago. We put our nose in places we had no business sniffing. I'm not willing to lose another American life over something the hearts of our people never wanted to be involved with in the first place. Tonight, I'm telling our people what they want to hear — the troops are coming home. We're not investing another five minutes guarding countries and sending billions of dollars to subsidize those who continually try to blow our brains out. Big business has led this dog and pony show for too many damn years. From now on, if American or European companies want to pull up roots from their own turf and plant them in Korea, Baghdad, Kuwait, Syria or Pangtantwo, they can hire their own security force to protect their asses. We're going to take the next four years building America back up. Hell, Harry, the money we spend overseas could feed and clothe every man, woman and child in America. It could pay for what America has been doing without for years — educational resources for our children, quality health care, debt reduction — don't get me started again on this — you know what's in my mind," the President said turning back to once again face his friend.

"Yes, Mr. President, I know. But you know that Europe is going to put up one hell of a fight about us pulling our troops from their soil and ditching all oil imports from the Mideast," the Chief of Staff quickly added.

"Our dependence on oil is going to be over. Let China, France and Germany chase those dogs," the President said.

"Mr. President, the fusion cell isn't ready — and won't be for another year or two."

"I won't stand for that, Harry. And once the public knows what's going on, I bet they'll pull those oil lobbyists out in the street and hang them out to dry if they try to tangle this program up in technical trials again. I intend to put it all out there — no more secrets. Fusion cells work —cars can go years without a single booster and there's no air pollution —something that will drive those bleeding heart environmentalists out of business on the Hill," the President said with just the hint of a smile. "Besides, we don't need oil from the Mideast to survive until this program is up and running — you know that — every man who has sat behind this high-powered desk has known that. Mexico and Canada can handle our needs beyond what we can't pipe up from our own wells and special reserve. We'll resource our refineries and drill on sites here that can pump enough of the black stuff until the fusion cells are in full production. I'm calling

J. Andy Murphy

in the markers as of tonight. It's time to give Allah his due. We don't belong in that part of the world — never have."

"Mr. President, you know I'm with you on this, but we have to be prepared for the actions Israel has to take."

"There's nothing really left of Israel, Harry, not the way it once was. Iran took care of that five years ago, remember? We can't even get close to helping them at this point. Besides, Israel's new alliance with Russia ties our hands. They're in a better position to make the calls now and Israel will do what it has to do," Grissam said, "this isn't coming as a big surprise to President Shirrel. I've told him of my intentions. He's just been waiting for me to make the call."

"They won't make it, Mr. President."

"I'm not ready to take that bet, Harry. They've been at war for hundreds of years — only this time, they have a few weapons at their disposal from the Russians that could once again part the waters," the President said.

"But will they use them?" Harry added.

"I'm sure they will this time as they have nothing to lose," the President said. The two men were silent for a few minutes. Each contemplating what was about to go down.

A smile suddenly jumped across Harry Corbett's face. "The media is going to crap their pants when they realize we pulled a bait and switch on them with your speech."

"The media is getting its' due, Harry," the President laughed, "won't that be something to see?" he quickly added.

"For the first time in fifteen years, the public will actually get to decide for themselves first what their own elected President actually said to them in a State of the Union address," the Chief of Staff mused.

"Isn't that the way it was really meant to be? Hell, the media has jacked the public around for so many years — it's like they think average people aren't smart enough to form their own opinions — that they have to be told by intellectual talking heads what the President just said. The truth is the media has danced to the tune of big corporate money and power for the last thirty years. Hollywood owns most of the major news divisions. News isn't news — it's an orchestrated puppet show. A few old white men control it all these days. They have their own agenda," the President stated tartly.

"You're not far off, Mr. President. God gives us heartache and the devil gives us the media," Cornett said with a look of disgust.

"Say, you haven't given me the names of the Take Aways. How come?" asked the President.

"Sorry about that, sir — Senator Elizabeth Tames, Congressman Drew Wharton and Assistant Undersecretary Jack November have been picked to go," Harry answered.

"Tames?" The President seemed surprised by this. "Harry. If we all go up in smoke over there tonight, Elizabeth Tames wouldn't know which end was up. She couldn't do the job under that kind of pressure."

"Neither could Congressman Wharton, Mr. President, but I don't think this is cause for concern," Cornett said as he stood up.

"Say, who is Jack November?" the President asked with a quizzical look on this face.

"Just some lucky schmuck who works for Caster," Harry answered.

The two men again fell into silent thought. Finally, Harry Corbett stood up. "Mr. President, you have about 45-minutes before show time. Do you want to spend some time alone?"

"Yeah. I could use a short break from all this. Give me the next 30 and then come get me," the President replied. "Make sure this text stays in your pocket. I don't want any slip up. Understood?"

"Understood, Mr. President."

Senator Elizabeth Tames' office was busy as usual. Her aides had placed the next day's work in her briefcase and added the list of calls she had to make from her home regarding fundraising issues. For some reason, Tames didn't feel all together today. Senate Majority Leader Kenneth Case had waited until nearly 11:30 p.m. to call her the night before with the news. She never really went back to sleep.

"Is your neck still bothering you, Senator?" Carrie Block, the senator's Chief of Staff asked.

"Yeah. It feels like a pinched nerve or something," the senator said without much inflection in her voice. "Did you make sure to pack the speech I'm giving on Saturday? I need to work on a few things — it just doesn't say all that I need to say," Tames questioned.

Yes, it's all there, plus, I put in the latest poll figures on the President that I think you should look at," Block added as she carefully placed one document after another in front of her Senator for signature purposes.

"I'm still amazed at how they go about the selection process for the "Take Away" thing," Tames said casually. "Frankly, I would have thought that someone higher up the food chain would have been given this role," she added casually.

"I think it's quite an honor, Senator Tames. I think it will show how well thought of you are —"

"Being well-thought of has nothing to do with this. My hunch is they took all the new kids on the block, put our names in a hat and Case drew one out — that being me," Tames said.

An assistant stuck her head in the door and announced that the Secret Service had just taken control of the office. Senator Tames gave one parting look to her long time friend. "I guess it is time, Carrie. I'll see you tomorrow — hopefully," she said with a nervous laugh.

"Senator, this question is probably way out of line, but have you given any thought to what you would do if something did happen and you were in charge?" Block asked with some hesitancy.

Elizabeth Tames straightened her shoulders and looked at Block for a few seconds. "I've given it some thought, Carrie, but only in passing. If something should happen on a catastrophic level that puts me in charge — well, I can only tell you that I'd hit back with everything we had. And then, I'd search for the last angry man still standing and personally shoot him on the spot. After that — I'd close our borders, lower our taxes and push for term limits. Yeah — I guess that about sums up what I'd do," Senator Tames said with no trace of a smile.

"You go girl," Carrie said with a kind of stunned look on her face.

"Are you ready, Senator Tames?" the Secret Service agent asked.

"I'm as ready as I'm ever going to be," she answered as she left her office and disappeared into the hallway surrounded by her escorts.

Congressman Drew Wharton walked briskly to the waiting unmarked car. Surrounded by Secret Service agents he imagined this to be the way the President felt every time he left the White House. He liked the feeling. Settling into the back seat of the SUV, equipped with bullet-proof glass, he quickly tried to make small talk with his escorts. He soon found out they were not about to engage in any small chatter with a Take-Away. They had a job to do and in this situation — they were totally in charge. They, too, enjoyed the feeling. Wherever he was going, though, was far better than where he had just left. His office was in turmoil as a major fundraiser for his last campaign was now being investigated by the State Attorney back home in his district. Congressman Wharton knew all too well how messy this was going to get, but right now — playing the game took some of the edge off the day.

"Can I make a few phone calls?" Congressman Wharton asked.

"I'm sorry, sir. All calls are now restricted," Agent Richard Andersen answered. "From now on, you are out-of-service, sir," he added.

"This must be old-hat to you guys?" Wharton said still trying to make conversation. The agent did not respond. "Are we picking up Senator Tames?" Wharton pressed.

"You're a single package, Congressman," the agent replied. Drew Wharton liked the powerful sound of that — a single package. In fact, Wharton liked anything that went with power.

The more power the better. He knew how to use it at this level and he could only imagine what it would be like at the next level — the highest level of all — the presidency. It gave him goose bumps just thinking about it.

Jack November was in the air. His escorts had arrived on time and the drive to the charter air field was made with no disturbance. He was nervous and he knew it showed in his face and his shaking hands. The agents were intimidating just because of who they were, and the job they were assigned to do on this special occasion. November didn't try to make conversation or ask any questions. He tried to keep his thoughts on his office and the five-thousand tasks that all needed his attention. He couldn't take any of that kind of work with him. Instead, he took a copy of the Constitution and a book on governmental law. He couldn't look out the chartered plane's windows because the shades were drawn and locked. All he knew was he was in the air and heading somewhere. Where were the others going? Would he end up where they were? The questions kept pressing him like an attack of gas from eating too much chili. Finally, Jack November did what he always did when things got too bent out of shape. He closed his eyes and fell asleep. Jack November was a token, and the good thing was, he knew it.

Harry Corbett didn't like what he was hearing. "What do you mean we have a lost signal from Seahorse," he asked.

"It's just a routine code match, sir. We have these all the time during field maneuvers. But it's in the book that you have to be notified when an atomic carrier —"

"So how long till you have this squared up?" Corbett interrupted as his deep blue eyes narrowed.

"I'm sure within the next hour, sir," the Navy liaison answered.

Harry Corbett turned and began the short walk from his office to the President's. Along the way, his thoughts kept him from returning eye contact with those that passed him.

Senior aides recognized the almost glazed look that the Chief of Staff often wore when deep in thought.

A slight knock on the door was immediately answered.

"Did you get any rest, sir?" Corbett asked.

"Some. Not enough," the President said as he stood in front of the mirror combing his salt and pepper close cropped hair. He had showered and changed into the customary dark blue suit. He looked fit and ready. "Is it time?"

"Yes, Mr. President. It is time," Corbett answered walking toward the door. As soon as he opened it, the President's personal agents entered the room.

"Well, Simon. Are you ready to walk your commander and chief to the car?" the President asked.

"Yes sir. We're ready to take you to the dance," Simon answered in his normal good humor tone.

As customary for such a state event, security was tight. The Senate and the House were locked down two hours before the President was to even enter their street address. An army of special agents went over every inch of the noble parlor where all the powerful people in government would gather to listen to their president discuss the pressing issues of the war-torn world. The small club of millionaire senators entered the room nodding to those they deemed worthy as they made their way to their seats.

The members of the House entered searching out the cameras and constantly reaching out to shake the hands of those that fed the machine that would return them to their thrones in the halls of Congress. When the room was filled with all those who marched to the beat of politics it contained the dusty aroma of power in a way that one must be present to smell. The President entered last to the roar of clapping hands and frozen smiles. He smiled broadly and then began to speak, quieting the gathered. The media, as expected, had spent the hour before dissing the prepared speech that had been delivered to their outlets earlier. Anchors for the major news networks were engaged in putting their spin into thoughtful comments that would so clearly deliver the message their studios wanted to get out.

When the President's words didn't match the speech in front of them they began to sweat beads of embarrassment that soon turned into full-blown anger. Harry Corbett could see the media anchors scrambling in their high perch above. A small smile was just barely in sight. God, how he loved the president for having the guts to do this. The funny thing about politics at this level was the hard cold truth that there was hardly ever any way to do something so original. President James Grissam had just begun his announcement of the all-troop pullout when everything the world knew as familiar and safe changed.

When the first blast hit there was no sound preceding it. Just a white flash of light. There was no time for terror to fill the heads of those who had survived the first hit as the second blast sealed their fate in just a matter of seconds. In less than five minutes, Senator Elizabeth Tames would be on her way from Camp David, her initial take away destination, to the disaster location appropriately named "Camp Survivor." Since the highest ranking military officers had also been obliterated in the attack, she was now surrounded by less seasoned personnel. When she arrived deep in the belly of the heavily fortified bunker she saw that state-of-the-art communication systems were in place.

"Senator Tames, you should be sworn in before we begin, but there's no time for formality as we've just entered a Amber Code and we need our acting President to give the order for immediate response," stated Mary Catherine Carter, a two-star general that had been put in place by the Chairman of the Joint Chiefs several months earlier.

"Do we know what happened?" Senator Tames asked.

"At this moment we do not have a clear picture. I can only tell you the attack came from — well, honestly, all we have is that it came from a runaway submarine somewhere off the East coast," she answered with beads of sweat gathering across her forehead.

"Do we know who was behind this yet, and if so, what is the plan for a counter attack?" she asked.

"The plan calls for retaliation at Code Red level," the General answered.

"What exactly is a Code Red level?" Tames asked impatiently.

"The orders are here in the black box, approved accordingly at the Executive level," General Carter answered as she set the metal box on the table between them.

"Where is Congressman Wharton?" Tames asked. "Shouldn't he be here with me?"

"I'm sorry. Congressman Wharton didn't make it."

"What? But he was a Take Away. He has to be safe," Tames responded with profound surprise.

"He was taken to a building near the White House and I'm afraid that area was also hit," the General answered shaking her head in after thought of such a plan.

"What all was hit? Do you have a report on that yet?" Tames asked.

"The House and Senate buildings were targets as were the White House and several national monuments," the General answered, adding, "New York was hit, as well as other key cities on the West coast, and more is coming in as we speak," the General said. "I'm afraid it is catastrophic," she added.

"Then let's open the damn box — wait. What happened to the other guy — the assistant Under —"

"Jack November. He's on his way, but it will take time to get him here. We don't think it's a good idea to have the two of you in the same zone for at least 24-hours."

"All right then, seems as if you and I don't have too much of a choice here. Let's get the box opened, General Carter," Tames said looking directly at the General with a bit of authority now present in her voice.

General Carter called for the protocol procedures and one-by-one they were enacted. Opening the box, the General spread the papers on the table. As they read their orders together, the room was completely silent. Senator Tames slowly sat down.

For a few seconds it appeared she might be sick as her skin coloring had turned to the shade of sour milk.

"Are you okay, Senator?" the General asked.

"Are you?" Tames replied acidly.

"I don't think anyone is ever going to be okay again if it means anything to you," General Carter answered."I'm sorry. Now isn't the time for this," Tames said recovering her composure.

"For clarity, we've identified that this launch was executed from China?" Tames asked.

"That's the pinpoint. It appears to be jointly fused with second assaults coming from the regions in the Mideast," The General answered.

"Okay then, I've read the orders and I agree with the outcome of such actions. By way of Executive Order, let's put this in play," Tames said in a level voice. The General reached across the table and touched Tames on the shoulder, "God help us all, Mrs. President — God help us all."

"Ironic isn't it, General?"

"I'm sorry, Mrs. President?"

"It's ironic because all this was started by men how many centuries ago, and now, it will be two women who end it," Tames said.

"Yes, madam, you have that right, but maybe we'll get a chance to change all that if we survive this," the General said matter-of-factly. With that, the plan went into effect. Long range missiles with atomic warheads were launched and the glow of death all across the world lit up the screens in the command center.

"Are you ready for the second launch, President Tames?"

"What's left?" the President asked staring at the screens.

"Very little," the General answered as she waited for the order to press the button signaling the last round of atomic devastation.

Elizabeth Tames, the last living President of the United States hesitated.

"Why? Can you tell me why we had to kill each other off in such an insane manner? How did we get here?"

"Mr. President, wake up — it's time for you to start getting ready," Harry Corbett said as he gently tried to stir the President from what was obviously a deep sleep.

"What? What the hell!" the President said as he sat straight up on the couch where he had laid down a little over 30-minutes ago.

"God, Harry. I've never been so glad to wake up in my life. I just had the scariest dream," the President said as he quickly stood up.

"Well, then I'm glad to have been the one to bring you back from that, sir," Corbett said as he handed the President a fresh cup of coffee with two sugars and no cream.

"Can I ask you what the dream was about, sir?" Corbett inquired.

"Let's just say that Senator Tames' is a lot more of a leader than I gave her credit for — and I'm glad it was only a dream."

"An unforetold prophecy of what's to come, sir?" Corbett asked.

"Let's hope it's not, my friend — let's hope it's not."

The End.

Printed in the United States
34792LVS00006B/112-165

9 781420 860153